Books by Sam Hamill

poetry

Heroes of the Teton Mythos
Petroglyphs
The Calling Across Forever
The Book of Elegiac Geography
Triada
animae
Fatal Pleasure
The Nootka Rose
Passport *(with Galen Garwood)*
A Dragon in the Clouds

poetry in translation

Night Traveling (from Chinese)
The Lotus Lovers: Visions of Tzu Yeh and Li Ch'ing-chao
The Same Sea in Us All (from the Estonian of Jaan Kaplinski)
Lu Chi's *Wen Fu* (The Art of Writing)
Catullus Redivivus (Selected Poems of Catullus)
Banished Immortal: Visions of Li T'ai-po
The Wandering Border (from the Estonian of Jean Kaplinski)
Facing the Snow: Visions of Tu Fu

essays

At Home in the World
A Poet's Work

FACING THE SNOW

FACING THE SNOW

Visions of Tu Fu

Translated by Sam Hamill

With calligraphy by Yim Yse

WHITE PINE PRESS

ISBN 0-934834-24-5

Acknowledgements:
   My deepest gratitude and admiration go to Yim Tse who "couldn't possibly accept money for writing out Tu Fu's poems." Thanks especially to P. S. Hansen, poet/painter/translator and formidable scholar, whose friendship and admonishments have been a constant throughout these years: *Ch'end hsin ch'eng i.*

   Thanks to the editors of the following journals, where many of these poems first appeared: *American Poetry Review, Cafe Solo, Floating Island, Loblolly, Poetry East, Stone Lion Review, Willow Springs.*
   Seven of these poems appeared in my *Night Traveling* (Turkey Press, 1985): "Dreaming of Li Po," "Night Thoughts While Traveling" (under the title "Night Traveling"), "Heavenly River," "In Praise of Rain," "A Summit," "Heading South," and a fragment from "The Journey North" (under the title "Traveling North).

—S.H.

Publication of this book was made possible, in part, by grants from the New York State Council on the Arts and the National Endowment for the Arts.

Design by Watershed Design.

Cover painting: Winter Landscape. Ch'ing Dynasty (1520) courtesy of the Freer Gallery of Art, Smithsonian Institution, Washington, D.C.

Printed in the United States of America.

WHITE PINE PRESS
76 Center Street
Fredonia, New York 14063

To William O'Daly and Lee Bassett;
to Kenneth O. Hanson and Denise Levertov;
to Harry and Sandra Reese;
and to the redoubtable Tree Swenson

CONTENTS

Introduction

Tu Fu was born in Honan in 712 AD, one hundred years after the founding of the T'ang Dynasty. His was a genteel family distinguished for its literary accomplishments, and there is some evidence to suggest Tu Fu may even have held several small farms of his own and may even have enjoyed a lifetime's modest income from these family holdings; but there is also contrary evidence suggesting convincingly that he suffered almost unbearable poverty, even to the extent of losing a child to famine. And the evidence of the poems themselves imply that he suffered both famine and exile with a strength of character few can even imagine.

Tu's early years seem to have been calm and reasonably happy ones. It was said during these years that one could travel ten thousand *li*, over a thousand miles, without need of a weapon. But while the country appeared to enjoy this period of relative peace, the Enlightened Emperor was handing over the reins of government to his prime minister, Yang Kuo-chung, a stupid and brutal man; simultaneously, the emperor was sponsoring and revelling in infamous debaucheries with his concubine, Yang Kuei-fei.

Despite his family's influence in literary circles and at the court, Tu was turned away from official appointment and from completion of his examinations until, at the age of forty-three, he was finally given a minor post without benefit of examination. But his time at the court was brief, owing largely to the moral bankruptcy of the court and internecine political intrigues that enveloped him.

Then, in 750, a long series of national disasters befell the Chinese, beginning with a year-long drought that devastated the harvests. The spring of 751 brought ever-increasing tragedy when a fleet of over two hundred grain cargo ships caught fire and burned; later that same year, China lost dominion over western Asia in the Battle of Samarkand; in the autumn, typhoons sank "several thousand ships" at the grain transport docks in Yangchow; during the same month, a fire devastated and destroyed the main arsenal in the capital at Ch'ang-an.

And as though the preceding two years of disasters were not sufficient to test the Chinese people, the typhoons of late 751 were only the beginning of two consecutive years of torrential rains which brought enormous floods and which once again destroyed the harvests. These natural disasters, combined with a growing public awareness of the emperor's decadence and the prime minister's cruelties, impoverished and embittered the people.

In 755, Tu made a short but difficult journey north from Ch'ang-an to visit his family in Feng-hsien, only to find upon arrival that his small son had died of malnutrition. About this same time, the rebel An Lu-shan brought an army from Beijing, crossed the Yellow River, and captured the eastern capital and Lo-yang, then, in early 756, declared the establishment of a new dynasty. Shortly thereafter, An Lu-shan invaded and sacked the capital at Chang-an.

Tu himself was captured during an attempt to flee, returned to the city, and spent nearly two years in the occupied capital. He had spent a total of nearly ten years there since arriving at the age of thirty-five. He had endured famine, and rejection by the court, and he had witnessed first-hand the appalling arrogance of the government.

Following the collapse of the An Lu-shan Rebellion, Tu was again given a sinecure, Court Censor, only to be once again turned out of office, a casualty of his own moral authority. In 759, broken, he became a wanderer, living in thatched-roofed huts in Szechuan until, old and ill, he attempted a final pilgrimage to the lands of his birth, only to perish on his boat in the struggle as he journeyed down the Yangtze River. He probably died of consumption.

One encounters time and again the idea that poetry in T'ang times was the realm of old men, mostly retired civil service literati. This is simply untrue. T'ang times were Confucian times, and since the root of Confucianism is filial piety, it was natural that many a poet would adopt the persona of the "long white-haired" old man—this lent a younger poet an authority of tone and diction he might never aspire to otherwise.

Tu's earliest reference to his own "long white beard" dates from somewhere between his nineteenth and twenty-fifth birthdays; by age thirty, he was certainly altogether comfortable speaking of his constant poverty, old age, and lack of recognition. And in doing so, he was well within the mainstream of poetics in his time, especially when we remember that poverty was considered honorable, and prosperity evil.

A proper Confucian gentleman, Tu also had a deep abiding respect for serious Taoists and Buddhists. His "reverence for life" which Kenneth Rexroth mentions is not limited to human life, but extends to all sentient beings. He is one of the most deeply religious poets without a formal religion in all of history. His poems cover the entire spectrum of human experience with the single exception of erotic poetry about women—even his wife is spoken of with Confucian formality—while writing some of the most memorable and remarkable poetry of friendship in any language. But whether writing political tracts in the guise of poetry, or composing poems confessing guilt over supporting war efforts, or extracting beautiful lyrics based upon the articulation of purely personal experience, Tu's voice reveals a deep abiding compassion.

There can be little doubt that the author of "Eight Immortals of the Wine-cup" was a frequent and enthusiastic imbiber. But he was no drunken Dylan Thomas falling down the stairs after schoolgirls. He favored a strong rice wine, thick, milky, and heady. And he knew how much was enough. As James J.Y. Liu points out in his study, *The Art of Chinese Poetry* (University of Chicago Press, 1962), the character *tsuei*, usually translated as "drunk," means "reaching the limit of capacity *without offending propriety*" (italics are my own). Many translators, reading frequent references to wine-drinking, fail to understand that these drinking parties were often also poetry-writing contests. Because they were a high point socially for poets who often went months, even years, without an opportunity for gathering with other poets, no one was reluctant to celebrate them.

But Tu was also fond of wine wherever and whenever he found it. And, sometimes, his wine, like his long white hair, is simply a conceit used to set a tone or frame a reference. Like the old man Eliot adopted as a persona while still in his twenties, Tu invented himself to some extent through his own personae, creating a world that exists today as it did then, altered only by our angle of perception.

Like William Carlos Williams, Kenneth Rexroth, and Denise Levertov in our own time, Tu was original, prolific, and largely unread by the public in his lifetime. His work was known, almost exclusively, by the few poets (including Li T'ai Po) who came under his influence. T'ang officialdom had its own official tastemakers much as we permit the unofficial tastemakers and contest organizers to run the Literature Busyness of our time. Tu Fu was, like Li T'ai Po and Meng Hao-jan, like Williams, Rexroth, and Levertov, a scholar out of office.

The first biography would not appear until nearly fifty years after his death, and most of his poetry simply disappeared for nearly three hundred years. Even now we have but twenty of his original sixty "bundles" of poetry and prose, a mere fifteen hundred poems, probably less than a third of what he wrote.

Tu wrote comfortably in all the forms and styles of his time. He also refined many of them. He is neither as "organic" a poet as Li Po, nor as stiffly formal as Li Ho. Nearly two-thirds of his extant poems are in the form of *lu-shih* or "regulated verse," an eight-line poem composed in five or seven syllable lines with the same rhyme used on even-numbered lines, and with parallel couplets used in lines 3/4 and 5/6. In Chinese, they are dense, lucid, allusive, and heavily cadenced mono-syllables.

Searching for a form in American English, I have chosen to respect Tu's line and couplet—that is, I have tried to say in a line what the original says in a line, but without attempting to do so by translating word for word, line by line. The couplet, in American speech, expresses something of the movement of the original, the pauses declared by caesurae and by the line itself, lightly end-stopped, the pauses not prolonged. In general, I have said what Tu said. Occasionally, I have seen fit to "translate" an image or reference as well. But it is unimportant whether these poems be considered "scholarly" by Sinologists. My aim has been, from the beginning some eleven years ago, to make accurate versions of the poems as *poems* in contemporary American language.

From the King James Bible to Dryden and on through Pound, Rexroth, Arrowsmith, and Keeley, the role of the translator has been constantly debated. I agree with Dryden (as, probably, with all of the above) that translation is primarily an act of sympathetic harmony: one finds in the voice of another an entrancing quality; one becomes enchanted; one takes that voice and those words into one's innermost being; one holds this inspiration until one is prepared to speak as an advocate for the original. While I cannot *be* Tu Fu, I must *speak* as Tu Fu.

Some of the best makers of poetry from the Chinese have been translators who knew little or nothing of the original: Judith Gautier, who got her cribs from a Thai collaborator whose own knowledge of Chinese was shaky at best; Ezra Pound, whose source, Ernest Fenollosa, got his crib from two Japanese who, in turn, had questionable ideas about Chinese poetry; Kenneth Rexroth, who began his brilliant versions of Chinese poems using Gautier's (among others') French as cribs.

If translation is indeed outright advocacy with its roots in sympathetic harmony, it is also the most severe apprenticeship. To quote from Rexroth's magnificent essay, "The Poet as Translator" (*Assays*, New Directions,1961): "Translation, however, can provide us with poetic exercise on the highest level. It is the best way to keep your tools sharp until the great job, the great moment, comes along. More important, it is an exercise of sympathy on the highest level. The writer who can project himself into the exultation of another learns more than the craft of words. He learns the *stuff* of poetry. It is not just his prosody he keeps alert, it is his *heart*. The imagination must evoke, not just a vanished detail of experience, but the *fullness* of another life." (All italics are my own emphasis.)

Furthermore, the "vanished details" and "fullness of another life" of which Rexroth speaks are not enough alone. "No poet, no artist of any art," T.S. Eliot says in a famous essay even the academies embrace, "has his complete meaning alone. His significance, his appreciation is the appreciation of his relation to the dead poets and artists. You cannot value him alone; you must set him, for contrast and comparison, among the dead. I mean this as a principle of aesthetic, not merely historical, criticism." Eliot goes on to explain that existing artistic monuments form an ideal order which is then modified with each new addition.

It should hardly be surprising then, to find that my Tu Fu is not unrelated to the Tu of Florence Ayscough, to the Tu of William Hung, and to the Tu of Rexroth, Irving Yucheng Lo, J.P. Seaton, Stephen Owen, and others. Where a previous translator has struck a particularly resonant chord, I have made use of that chord, but have stolen it in part as a gesture of friendship, a courteous and happily acknowledged theft of which I believe old Mr. Tu would approve.

Friendship is surely Tu's greatest attribute. As Arthur Waley pointed out many years ago, the Western poet declares himself a lover; the

Chinese poet offers friendship. Tu Fu and Li T'ai Po are about as opposite as any two poets may be; and yet, although they probably met but once, Tu wrote his friend Li a number of poems and also composed a number about him. But even in his poems of praise and friendship, Tu could bury a needle—writing of his elder in "To Li Po on a Spring Day," Tu praises Li very highly ("There's no one quite like you," or more literally, "Po it is!"), echoing the praise of Confucius for his own disciple, Yen Hui (*Analects* VI.9). Thus, upon close reading, we find the poet has addressed his elder in an echo of Master Kung speaking to a disciple. [Stephen Owen examines this poem at some length in his *Traditional Chinese Poetry and Poetics* (University of Wisconsin Press, 1985) along with a number of other poems by Tu Fu.]

Along with the shorter poems of friendship, family, and nature, I have included several political/historical poems, most notably "The Journey North," one of the longest poems of the T'ang Dynasty and one which relates the terrible struggles during the An Lu-shan Rebellion. He was a bitter opponent of conscription (see "The Draft Board at Shih-hao" and "Peng-ya Road") who witnessed not only heart-breaking imperial excesses, but the rages of warfare and the ravages of nature. He was happiest among "the best people [he] can find anywhere: woodcutters and fishermen." He felt "the essential goodness" of the poor. In Shensi, Kansu, and Szechuan, he wandered through freezing seasons along treacherous roads and trails among desperate men in desperate times, a lonely voice of sanity among the voiceless and the victimized during a rebellious, feudal time.

Rexroth said he was perhaps the greatest non-epic, non-dramatic poet who ever lived. Where I have occasionally strayed from either his titles or his exact words, I have done so primarily to remain true to the spirit of his poems. His poems, so rich in place-names and allusion, euphemism, double entendre and the like, evitably get, in translation, "dumbed down." Even so, he speaks today for our time just as surely as he spoke then for his own. Faced with a final choice, I would choose the spirit over the word in translating a poem from any tongue. Reading poetry in translation, one has a right to expect exactitude only in the language given. What deadens most translation (especially from a language as different from our own as classical Chinese) is the inexact language that "retains something of the original" while supplying only platitudes, cliches, or dull prose in the language given.

"The greatest infidelity," John Frederick Nims has written, "is to pass off a bad poem in English as representing a good one in another language . . . It should be unnecessary to remind ourselves yet again that poetry is less a matter of *what* is said than of *how* it is said." In so saying, he echoes Valery's dictum: "Fidelity to meaning alone is a kind of betrayal."

Four hundred years after Tu Fu, Yang Wan-li addressed the nature of poetry:

"Now, what is poetry?
If you say it is simply a matter of words,
I will say a good poet gets rid of words.
If you say it is simply a matter of meaning,
I will say a good poet gets rid of meaning.
'But,' you ask, 'without words and without meaning,
where is the poetry?'
To this I reply: 'Get rid of words and get rid of meaning,
and there is still poetry.' "

(translated by Jonathan Chaves in his *Heaven My Blanket, Earth My Pillow*, Weatherhill Books)

and Yangs comments apply equally to poetry in translation. Even Horace warned against the *verbum verbo* method.

Much of Tu Fu is found in his powerful dyanamics. But North American English does not make the sounds of Chinese. Our language hasn't the compression. It is far less inclined toward natural rhyme. Through the line and the image and the sound, I have addressed the tone of the original, and in doing so consistently, I have perhaps turned the poem away from what some might think of as the original intent. But I do not believe poetry has intention except in the most general way, just as all poetry is autodidactic in a general way. The poem is its own occasion, and is "translation" even into the original language. Tu Fu often makes a juxtaposition, only to follow it with a sigh of recognition. My impersonation attempts to revitalize his methods.

My beginning trots were of my own making, mostly from poems I already knew from other translators. These first literals were often corrected or emended or explicated by anyone whose knowledge of Chinese I respected. Where poems have been previously translated, I studied the existing translations. I have addressed Tu's forms by translating the techniques more often than the syllabic count, retaining his couplets and his parallelism whenever possible, for the juxtaposition that results in parallel structure often embodies the true experience of the poem. But even my use of "parallelism" is not the same as in the original—in the Chinese, it is a strict *syntactical* parallelism, whereas my adaptation is imagistic parallelism which approaches, indeed recognizes, the original syntax without attempting to re-create it. Finally, I simply threw out all notation and revised the manuscript as a whole, for, as I have stated, it is my intention to present a "Tu Fu" —that is, a book written by a human being.

There are no footnotes to these poems. William Hung's *Tu Fu: China's Greatest Poet* provides an adequate biography and fairly literal prose renderings of many poems. Aforementioned titles by James J.Y. Liu and Stephen Owen provide a suitable introduction to Chinese poetics. Indeed, Western culture is at long last beginning to discover classical Chinese culture, and the many commentaries and translations of scholars like Burton Watson are so readily available that I feel abbreviated footnotes would only detract from the poems themselves; nor is it my intention to provide hopelessly reductive notes for poems which indeed should speak themselves. I have retained the Wade-Giles system for transliteration of Chinese because it indicates aspiratives (indicated with an accent ') missing in Pinyin.

I am grateful to P.S. Hansen for his patient tutelage and for his assistance in obtaining texts for the study of Chinese, and Chinese texts themselves, as for his exegesis of any number of complex characters. Prof. Irving Yucheng Lo has been most generous with his time and scholarship and magnaminous in spirit, and this volume would certainly be less accurate without his scrupulous reading of my text in draft, and without his shrewdly insightful and incisive comments. And Prof. J.P. Seaton has likewise provided insights and encouragement for which I am grateful.

Were it not for the generosity of the John Simon Guggenheim Memorial Foundation, this volume might never have been completed. And were it not for the sustaining faith and generosity of my partner, Tree Swenson, it surely would never have come to fruition.

I offer this toast to a kindly old master, unlettered and unsung in his lifetime: a few poems to be chanted, accompanied by a cup of milky, strong rice wine.

Sam Hamill

1976-88
Moon Watching Pavilion
Port Townsend
Year of the Dragon

FACING THE SNOW

Sunset

How beautiful the river is in spring
with sunset filling the window.

The garden on the bank is sweet,
and so is the smoke of the boatmen.

Sparrows squabble in the branches,
insects buzz through my court.

Ah, heady unstrained wine—one cup
and a thousand griefs will vanish.

Random Pleasures (I)

A dragon sleeps three winter months,
the old crane longs to fly a thousand miles.

The ancients we admire
were as foolish as we are now.

Hsi K'ang died too young,
but K'ung-ming found one admirer.

They are like two hillside pines:
their use determines their worth.

In winter snow, their trunks impress,
but soon they, too, will fall.

Random Pleasures (II)

T'ao Ch'ien withdrew from all the world,
but he could not find the Way.

Reading through his poems now,
I find him always complaining.

He struggled all his life,
his gift did not come early.

His sons were wise or foolish,
but why should T'ao Ch'ien worry?

Rising Spring Waters

The river's up two feet overnight.
No way these banks can hold it.

Near the market, there are boats for sale.
If I had money, I could buy one

and moor it at my gate.

Evening Near Serpent River

Breezes sigh, rising over bright tiled steps,
the round sun sinks below the wall.

Wild autumn geese slowly vanish
as sunset lengthens all the clouds.

Leaves have begun to drop already.
Cold flowers lose their fragrance.

I add my tears to the river.
At slacktide, only the moon is pure.

Descending Through Dragon Gate

The river drops from Dragon Gate
between walls of marked granite.

High winds kick up high waves
that have tossed ten thousand years.

The pathway veers and winds,
blown like a single thread.

This shaky bridge is hung
from hand-chipped nooks in rock.

My eyes float down like falling petals.
Misty rain whistles through my hair.

My whole life hangs in the balance:
one slip and it's all over.

I've heard of other fearsome trails,
and some I've had to try.

But whatever I think is dangerous
I'll measure against this climb.

Dragon Gate Gorge

Dragon Gate cuts a wide gorge.
Trees line the road from the city gate,

and the Imperial Palace is imposing.
The temples are silver and gold.

The seasons shift. I come and go,
the lands and waters roll on.

Of all those I met along this road,
will I ever meet any again?

Yen-chou City Wall Tower

I came east to pay a son's respects,
and now I look out from South Tower:

clouds reach from T'ai-shan to the eastern sea,
and a great plain covers Ch'ing and Hsu.

There was a monument to a tyrant on that peak,
and ruins lie where a kind prince ruled a city.

I have always valued antiquity.
Let others go on home. I will remain alone.

Looking at Mount T'ai

T'ai-shan is a holy place
reflecting the green of the plains,
home of a thousand mysteries and more.
Dawn and dusk are born here in a moment.

Gathering clouds erase the unreal world.
The birds sail slowly out of sight.
Like Master Kung, I'll climb to the summit
and watch all other mountains dwindle.

Leaving Ch'in-chou

The old monastery north of the city
was once a famous palace.

Now moss and lichens grow on the temple gate
and the red-green palace hall stands empty.

The moon is bright, the dew heavy,
and winds push clouds along the river.

Wei River flows steadily east without feeling.
I am alone with my sorrow.

Passing Mr. Sung's Old House

Mr. Sung's old house collapses.
The pond is full of moss.

I wandered here as a boy,
and was invited to leave a poem.

Old neighbors tell me stories now
until we lapse, at last, into silence.

The old oak looms like an aging general.
Sunset. Winds grieve its trembling leaves.

Visiting the Monastery at Lung-men

I explored the grounds with monks this evening,
and now the night has passed.

Heavy silence rises all around us
while late moonlight spills through the forest.

The mountain rises almost into heaven.
Sleeping in the clouds is cold.

A single stroke of the early prayer-bell wakes me.
Does it also waken my soul?

Going to the Palace with a Friend at Dawn

The water-clock marks dawn,
the peach blossoms rosy as wine.

Dragons and snakes on banners snap in the warm morning sun.
Sparrows and swallows glide on palace breezes.

I can smell the palace incense on your sleeve.
Poems should drip from your brush like pearls.

Who influence the Court for more than one generation?
Another pheasant feather floats in the palace pool.

Taking Leave of Two Officials

At the Government Office Building,
wu-t'ung trees shade the empty courtyard.

Beaten by public office, you finally return to your home.
To stay or leave? Thinking breaks my springtime mood.

The palace walls will divide us
and clouds will bury the hills.

All men long for noble horses.
But don't let old age catch you unprepared.

To Li Po on a Spring Day

There's no poet quite like you, Li Po,
you live in my imagination.

You sing as sweet as Yui,
and still retain Pao's nobility.

Under spring skies north of the Wei,
you wander into the sunset

toward the village of Chiang-tung.
Tell me, will we ever again

buy another keg of wine
and argue over prosody and rhyme?

River Pavilion

I lie out flat on the river pavilion
reciting poems or dreaming.

Water roars by, but my heart grows still.
Clouds drift over and my mind responds lazily.

Nothing moves in springtime dusk.
Such joy in the secret wants of things.

How can I retire to my forest home again?
To dispel my melancholy, I write another poem.

Random Pleasures (III)

All day, all night, I worry,
wondering over my brother.

Alive or dead, I cannot know,
so many roads between us.

The rebels broke our lines, we scattered.
Now we starve and freeze, looking for each other.

I long for the squeak of my farmhouse gate,
but fear the wolves and tigers may find me.

Each bird and beast has its place:
high up, cloudy, a single line of geese.

Random Pleasures (IV)

Blown by winds, the thistledown
drifts where it will, falling

through a thousand feet of frozen sky
to find another world.

The crooked path to my old home
has been deserted three long years.

Far off, the beacon flares blaze up—
chariots and weapons flood the eastern pass.

How long is one man's time on earth?
How long must the life of a wanderer last?

After Rain

At Heaven's border, the autumn clouds are thin
and driven from the west by a thousand winds.

The world is beautiful at dawn after rain,
and the rains won't hurt the farmers.

Border willows grow kingfisher green,
the hills grow red with mountain pears.

A Tartar lament rises from the tower.
A single wild goose sails into the void.

車轔轔，馬蕭蕭，行人弓箭各在腰。耶娘妻子走相送，塵埃不見咸陽橋。牽衣頓足攔道哭，哭聲直上干雲霄。道傍過者問行人，行人但云點行頻。或從十五北防河，便至四十西營田。去時里正與裹頭，歸來頭白還戍邊。邊庭流血成海水，武皇開邊意未已。君不聞漢家山東二百州，千村萬落生荊杞。縱有健婦把鋤犁，禾生隴畝無東西。況復秦兵耐苦戰，被驅不異犬與雞。長者雖有問，役夫敢申恨。且如今年冬，未休關西卒。縣官急索租，租稅從何出。信知生男惡，反是生女好。生女猶得嫁比鄰，生男埋沒隨百草。君不見青海頭，古來白骨無人收。新鬼煩冤舊鬼哭，天陰雨濕聲啾啾。

丙寅立夏漢一首　杜甫兵車行　謝瑨書

Song of the War Wagons

Wagons clang and horses cry
as soldiers pass with bows and arrows.
Families clamor to watch them go.
A huge cloud of dust swallows the trembling bridge.
Clinging to their clothes, they weep and stumble by,
their cries echoing through the sky.

And if you questioned them, they would say,
"Conscripted at fifteen, we fought for the north;
now almost forty, we move to fight in the west.
Once, villagers gave us honors,
now we return white-haired, heading toward frontiers.
We've shed a sea of blood.
Still the emperor wants more.
East of the mountains, a thousand villages,
ten thousand villages, turn to bitter weeds.
Even when strong women work the fields,
our canals and crops are feeble.
The warriors of Ch'in fight on,
driven like dogs and cattle.

You may ask, but we don't dare complain.
This winter we await new troops
while officials raise new taxes.
But where will the money come from?
We've learned the grief of raising sons—
not like the quiet joy of daughters
we can marry to our neighbors.
Our boys lie under the weeds.
Near Kokonor, their old white bones
remain with no one to collect them.
Old ghosts and new complaints: you can hear them
all night long through falling mist and rain.

The Draft Board at Shih-hao

As I was lodged at Shih-hao one night,
the draft board came for inductees.

While his wife delayed them at the gate,
one old man slipped over his wall and away.

The senior officer, in a rage,
cursed the woman into tears,

and then I heard her speak:
"All three of our sons went off to war.

And now a single letter returns—
two sons dead on the battlefield,

one on his last life's breath.
The dead are lost forever.

There's no one left at home
but a grandson nursing mother's breast,

too young to leave her side.
And she so poor her skirts are made of patches.

Although my strength has long since flown,
take *me* tonight, I beg you,

and I'll go to Ho-yang
and cook you all your breakfast."

The night and the voices passed,
except for the woman's sobbing.

I turned to the trail, first light breaking behind me
as the old man bid farewell to his family.

To Li Po on a Winter Day

Alone in my secluded hut,
I think of you all day, Li Po.

Whenever I read of friendship,
I remember your friendly poems.

Harsh winds tatter your old clothes
as you search for the wine of endless life.

Unable to go with you, I remember only
that old hermitage we'd hoped to make a home.

Moon on the Cold Food Festival

Homeless on Cold Food Festival Day,
I have nothing but this river of my tears.

If I cut down the moon's one cassia tree,
wouldn't the moonlight be brighter?

When red flowers bloom for lonely lovers,
her brow will be knit by sorrows.

No complaints. Like Cowboy and Weaving Girl,
we'll cross the river in autumn.

Moonlit Night

This same moon hangs over Fu-chou.
Alone, she'll lean out her window to watch it.

Our poor children are too small
to even remember Chang-an.

Dew will dampen her perfumed hair.
Clear moonlight makes her bare arms cool.

Will we ever sit again in her window,
the tears finally gone from our faces?

Lament for Ch'en T'ao

The first month of winter the blood of sons
of all the families flowed like water through Ch'en T'ao Marsh.

The whole country empty, sky clear, quiet,
forty thousand died here on a single afternoon.

Barbarians return with arrows dipped in blood,
drunk in the streets, howling Barbarian songs.

We turn our eyes away and cry toward the north
praying night and day the imperial army will come.

Word from My Brothers

Word arrives from far P'ing-yin—
my brothers are still alive.

They traveled hard to far villages
searching for supplies.

But even there, the fires of war
are blazing up again.

Fresh tears fall on the fallen:
infirmity, old age, . . .

how can I possible know
whether I'll ever see them again?

Passing the Night

Flowers beside the palace fade,
the sun sinks into the hills.

Last birds sing their way back home
and the first stars faintly shimmer

over a thousand palace doors.
The moon is huge and round.

Awake in the night, I listen
for the tinkle of keys in locks

like jade bridle-bells
set ringing in the wind.

At my dawn audience, they'll ask,
"I trust your night was peaceful?"

Poem for Mr. Li in Early Spring

Though sick, I rise at dawn—
your poem, Grief in Early Spring, has come.

It multiplies the autumns in my heart
and I realize old age has found me.

Tender peach-buds all blush red,
the willow shoots turn green.

Night after night, I dream of home, but
within Four Seas, only the dust and the wind.

Farewell Rhyme

Reluctant, I must take leave from war
to tend my ailing garden.

But before the journey, this poem of goodby.
We'll lighten our sadness with wine.

Rain fell hard all through the fall,
and now the weather is clearing.

Climbing mountain trails, I'll hear war bugles everywhere,
but how will I bear their calling?

P'eng-ya Road

I remember fleeing the rebels
through dangerous northern canyons,

the midnight moon shining bright
on narrow P'eng-ya Road.

So poor we went on foot,
we were embarrassed meeting strangers.

A few birds sang in the valleys,
but we met no one ever returning.

My daughter was so starved she bit me,
she screamed her painful hunger.

I clamped her mouth shut tight,
fearful of wolves and tigers.

She struggled hard against me,
she cried and cried.

My son was sympathetic
and searched the wilds for food.

Then five days of heavy rain arrived,
and we trudged through freezing mud.

We had no coats, no shelter,
we were dressed in cold, wet clothes.

Struggling, struggling, we made
but a mile or two each day.

We ate wild fruits and berries,
and branches made our roof.

Mornings we slogged through water,
evenings we searched for smoke on the skyline.

We stopped at a marsh
to prepare our climb to the pass,

and met a Mr. Sun
whose standards are high as clouds.

We came through the dark
and lamps were lit, gates opening before us.

Servants brought warm water
so we could bathe our aching feet.

They hung paper banners
in our honor.

Mrs. Sun came out with all her children.
They wept for our condition.

My children slept, exhausted,
until we roused them with food.

Our host took a vow
he'd always remain my brother.

His home was made our home,
to provide for every comfort.

Who could imagine in such troubled times
he'd bare his heart and soul?

A year has passed since that fated night.
The Barbarians still wage war.

If I had the wings of the wild goose,
I'd fly to be at his side.

The Journey North

On the first day, Eighth Moon,
autumn in our Lord's second year,

I travel north searching for my family,
enquiring everywhere under this blue, blank sky.

Welcomed at Court or cast out, no man
these days has time for leisure.

Humbled by Imperial favor, I return by decree
to my poor thatched hut in the mountains.

I linger at the Palace Gate signing out,
overcome with fears and doubts—

I always seem to fall short of my mark—
I mustn't ignore my duty to my Lord.

Our Lord has made a Renaissance,
he is so compassionate, so just.

To the east, Barbarians persist in rebellion.
I am torn between my duties.

Tearful, I long for Traveling Palace.
My journey begins in confusion.

The whole world is walking wounded,
but the savagery continues.

I make my slow, lonely way across
a devastated land—not even smoke

from a fire—and the few I meet are casualties,
wounds bleeding. They groan and they weep.

Turning toward Feng-hsiang,
camp banners flutter in faint light.

I climb the cold trail into mountains,
crossing endless empty campgrounds.

The Pin-chou Plain sinks below,
Ching River rolling on and on.

A wild tiger springs before me:
his roar could shatter granite.

Wild autumn flowers wilt.
Wagon-ruts scar the road.

Climbing into clouds, my spirits rise.
Here is contemplation, here is solace.

There are chestnuts and acorns
and wild berries everywhere,

some as red as cinnabar,
some as black as lacquer.

They have rain and dew from heaven,
and grow sweet or tart by nature.

Homesick for the Peach Blossom Spring,
I regret my tribulations even more.

From this high trail, I see the Fu-chou hills,
and canyons and mountains beyond them.

My servant high behind me in the trees,
I rush down to meet the river.

Owls cry in the mulberry trees,
the field mice ready for winter.

We cross the battleground at midnight:
cold moonlight falls on frozen bones.

Ten thousand men enlisted at T'ung-kuan,
now ten thousand men are gone.

Who destroyed the clans of Ch'in,
who murdered half our men?

When I dreamed I fell in Barbarian dust,
it turned my dark hair white.

It's taken a year to reach my hut
and find my poor wife in rags.

Seeing me, she cries like wind through pines
and weeps a stream of tears.

My boy who brightened my life
is pale as winter snow.

He turns to hide his tears.
His bare feet scuff the dust.

My girls stand by the bed in tatters,
their dresses barely reaching to their knees.

Ocean waves embroidered on my old robe
were cut into mismatched patches,

sea-dragon and purple phoenix severed
to repair their shabby clothes.

A poor scholar, I agonize,
and lie three days in bed and vomit.

My bag holds one small blanket—
I can't even warm my family.

I unwrap a little rouge and powder,
and then unfold the blanket.

My poor wife's face slowly brightens
and my girls brush out their hair,

giggling, imitating their mother,
rouge splotched on cheeks,

powder in their eyes and hair,
eyebrows painted crooked.

It makes this poverty almost enough
returning home alive.

They question, tugging my beard for attention,
and I haven't the heart to stop them.

I tolerate rough, noisy children
remembering the grief brought by rebellion.

Finally reunited, at last I can console them,
but how can I support them?

Even our Lord must eat the dust of exile.
Who knows when the killing will ever end?

I search the skies for a sign
and all the heavens shudder.

Cold winds howl from the north,
along the Uighur trails,

delaying the day we'll be rescued
by the Uighur charge to the front.

The Uighurs number five thousand troops
with ten thousand horses before them.

They don't require great numbers,
preferring surprise attack.

Quietly vicious like circling hawks,
they're quicker than well-placed arrows.

After debate and confusion,
our Lord has chosen to trust them.

Soon, we'll regain Lo-yang,
then the capital at Ch'ang-an.

The Imperial Army marches east
to set a major ambush.

Recapturing both towns,
they'll also retake the mountains.

Winter darkens the heavens.
This is death's long season.

The year will judge the Barbarians,
the months will crush the Tartars.

Since they cannot escape their fate,
our best years lie ahead.

We endured the evil princes of antiquity
and of the recent past;

we quartered vile officials
and exiled their hired thugs;

Hsia and Yin were ended
at the hands of evil women;

Chou and Han were wounded,
but lived to rise again.

Praise our General Ch'en —
he inspires as he leads.

Through him, we'll have a second life;
without him, our nation might have perished.

The Great Hall waits, empty and cold;
no one lingers at the gate.

But soon we'll regain lost splendor
as our Lord names a Golden Court.

Sent to the Magistrate of P'eng-chou

A hundred years, and half have passed already.
Autumn arrives with its cold and hunger.

I wonder after the Prefect of P'eng-chou: when
will I be rescued from all my present hardships?

国破山河在 城春草木深 感时花溅泪 恨别鸟惊心 烽火连三月 家书抵万金 白头搔更短 浑欲不胜簪

杜工部春望 陈辉

Another Spring

In all the country,
only the landscape is firm.
It is springtime in the city.
Weeds cover everything, the trees
are overgrown, the flowers are watered
with our tears, until even the birds
have learned to moan.

Beacon fires of war
have lit the hills for months.
I'd give anything for a letter.
I scratch my poor white head
and hair falls out,
and my hair's already so thin
it can barely hold a hairpin.

Leaving Government Offices

It is spring and almost dawn when the crowds gather
near the court with all their banners.

Flowers drop their petals as I retire from Court.
Willows open their leaves.

Snowmelt dampens the walls.
Clouds cover the palace, darkening the halls.

Alone, in secret, I burn my draft memorial.
In my saddle, I yearn for a rooster's perch.

Drinking at Crooked River

Beyond the park, at River's Head,
the water's calm, the palace disappears.

Peach and willow blossoms scatter
as orioles fly up together.

Drinking, I don't care what they say—
I never cared for the courts.

From my office I now see the immortals
have long since sunk into the sea.

Old and grieved, I see it's futile
to lament the duties I evaded.

Crooked River Meditation

Each falling petal diminished spring.
Ten thousand of them sadden me.

Spring flowers pale, and I grieve,
and ease my remorse with wine.

Kingfishers nest in the temple hall,
there is a stone unicorn on a royal grave.

Taking my pleasures where I find them,
I fill my cup again.

Drinking with Elder Cheng the Eighth at Crooked River

At River's Head, birds swarm through willow flowers.
Marsh birds and wild ducks commingle.

But spring holds nothing for two old men,
just our wine jar and remembrance.

Those beside the Emperor, even now, can't find a place of their own.
How can this old body no longer have a home?

You are still a tower of strength. How could you
even think of planting melon seeds beside a mansion gate?

死别已吞声，生别常恻恻。江南瘴疠地，逐客无消息。故人入我梦，明我长相忆。恐非平生魂，路远不可测。魂来枫林青，魂返关塞黑。君今在罗网，何以有羽翼。落月满屋梁，犹疑照颜色。水深波浪阔，无使蛟龙得。

Dreaming of Li Po

I.
Parted by death, we'd strangle on our tears;
parting in life, we've memories to cling to.

There is pestilence south of the river,
you are exiled, and I have not a word.

Old friend, I see you only in dreams,
but you know my heart is with you.

It's not the same as having your living spirit:
that road's too long to be measured.

Your spirit is in the heart of green maple,
your spirit returns to the dark frontier.

Tangled in nets of law, tell me,
how can the spirit soar?

Moonlight fills my room. Your poor face
shines, reflected in the rafters.

The waters are deep, the waves wide.
May peaceful serpents pass you by.

浮雲終日行遊子久不至三夜頻夢君情親見君意告歸常局促
苦道來不易江湖多風波舟楫恐失墜出門搔白首若負平生志
冠蓋滿京華斯人獨憔悴孰云網恢恢將老身反累千秋萬歲
名寂寞身後事

丙寅暮春錄杜甫夢李白二首　謝琰

II.
All day, huge clouds roll by.
You, exile, must travel.

Three nights I dreamed of you,
I dreamed we were together.

"I try, I try," you say, "but
this bitter road is difficult to travel:

winds drive lakes and rivers into waves,
my boat and oars would fail."

Leaving, you smoothed your long white hair
like a man who embraced his failures.

In Ch'ang-an, they lavish praise on officials
while you endure and endure.

They say that Heaven's net is wide.
We're tangled in the web of aging.

Your fame will last ten thousand years
though you are silent, vanished from this world.

To Abbot Min the Compassionate

Has it really been thirty years?
Writing this, I can't choke back the tears.

Are you still the servant of culture?
And who can an old man sing to?

Who packs your heavy Go board up the hill?
I remember your robe as our boat drifted on the water.

Now, they say, I've a future in office.
Me, a white old head dozing, drinking, dozing off again.

Heavenly River

Heavenly River is muddy year-round
except in the clarity of autumn

when a few small clouds make shadows,
but it's always bright at night.

The stars that swim the river shine on the capital dome.
The river carries off the moon to set beyond the border.

Cowboy and Weaving Girl cross the river each autumn
and neither wind nor wave can stop them.

Thinking of Li Po

A cold wind out of the wilderness.
What would you recommend?

When will the wild goose bring news
from the Lakes-and-Rivers land?

Poets must live without success,
driven by their daemons.

Remember the ghost of poor Ch'u Yuan—
send him a poem down the river.

Watching the Distances

I watch the limitless distance of autumn,
the far-off dark rising up in layers

where icy waters merge with the frozen sky
and the city is blurred with mist.

Last leaves are torn into flight by winds,
and sunless, distant peaks fade fast.

A lone crane flops home at dusk.
The trees are already full of crows.

Ch'iang Village

Western clouds, hill above hill,
vermillion poured over the sunset,
and the sun walks into the earth.
Birds sing everywhere at my hermitage
as I return, suddenly old and weary.

It's a wonder I survive.
My wife and children weep.
The winds have blown me away
and waves have washed me back.
I'm lucky to be alive.

Neighbors swarm over our wall
sighing, crying and carrying on.
Red-eyed with our tears,
we light the evening candle—
together we enter the dream.

The Cricket

The cricket is so small a thing,
yet moves us with tender chirping—

so quiet out among the weeds,
now it's crept under our bed to sing.

Its song brings an aging pilgrim tears,
it keeps the lonely wife awake.

Neither guitar nor flute can sing
as sweetly as natural music.

Listless

I can't bear a journey to the village—
I'm too contented here.
I call my son to close the wooden gate.

Thick wine drunk in quiet woods, green moss,
jade gray water under April winds—
and beyond: the simmering dusk of the wild.

Firefly

You who are born in decay
dare not fly into the sun.

Too dim to light a page,
you spot my favorite robe.

Wind-tossed, you're faint beyond the curtain.
After rain, you're sparks inside the forest.

Caught in winter's heavy frost,
where can you hide, how will you resist it?

Sick Horse

Old horse, I've pushed you hard
through frontier snow and ice.

Now the autumn dust exhausts you,
you grow old, and stubborn, and sick.

You were never much to brag about,
but you kept your spirits high.

Now you suffer your last humility,
and all I can do is sigh.

Empty Purse

Tasted, the green cypress is bitter.
Morning clouds are high, but can be eaten.

My generation sold itself for money,
but my way has not been easy:

a cold stove, a well of solid ice,
thin clothes and a cold bed at night.

My empty purse is embarassed.
I leave it my last thin penny.

Departing from Ch'in-chou

As old age weakens me, I grow lazy and foolish.
I make no plans for the future.
Hungry, I remember a land of plenty;
cold, I recall the warmth of the south.
In early November, Han-yuan
is cool and crisp like autumn,
but leaves have not turned yellow and fallen,
and the landscape is still lovely.
Chestnut Station promises good fortune,
and the plains are thick with farms
growing delectable yams
and wild honey and forests of bamboo shoots.
There are shimmering ponds for fishing.
Although my wanderings have grieved me,
this journey restores my country spirit.

But so many people pass through Ch'in-chou,
I fear I'll become entangled—
appalling social functions
and touring won't assuage my worries.
No ominous boulders shadow these ravines,
and these sandy farms grow smaller.
How can I possibly linger
where nothing brings an old man peace?

The lonely lookout post was swallowed by the dark.
Ravens cry from the city walls.
We depart at night in our carts, our horses
pausing to drink at the ponds.
The moon and stars rise clear
above the mist and clouds
reaching the endless void of space.
Before me, the way goes on forever.

Impromptu

We descend on horses onto the battleground.
The emptiness is wide.

Winds moan in the clouds,
yellow leaves blow by my feet.

On anthills among tangled grasses
lie a thousand shattered bones.

Passing by, the old people can only sigh,
while the young want another front.

Between the Han and the Huns, alternate wins and losses:
the frontier's never secure.

How can I find a good general so our armies
can enjoy a quiet night of sleep?

Song of T'ung-ku

Already old, and still without a name,
I've starved three years in these mountains.

The ministers of Ch'ang-an all are young,
their money and honors earned.

My friends, the mountain sages,
dwell only on the past, in their hurting.

I chant this last song sadly, my eyes
on the August sky where the white sun races.

Becoming a Farmer

Brocade City lies in dust and smoke.
This river village has only a dozen houses.

Lotuses spread their leaves and float,
the good wheat bends from its weight.

Here, far from the capital,
I will farm till I am old.

Ko Hung sought immortality in cinnabar,
but here I will meet my fate.

清江一曲抱村流 長夏江
村事事幽 自去自來堂上
燕 相親相近水中鷗
老妻畫紙為棋局 稚子
敲針作釣鉤 多病所須
唯藥物 微軀此外復
何求

杜甫 江村 謝琰

In a Village by the River

The clear river curves around our village:
these long summer days are beautiful, indeed.

Swallows swoop from the eaves,
the gulls all flock to the water.

My wife draws a rice-paper Go board
while our sons bend fish-hooks from needles.

This medicine is all a sick man needs.
What man could ask for more?

The Servant Boy Delivers

The pears are green as new jade,
plums and apricots slowly turning yellow.

My boy comes quiet to the garden
bearing his basket of fruit.

Soft winds bring a heady fragrance,
the plums still drip with dew.

All for this lazy guest of lakes and rivers
as long days lengthen into years.

Early Rising

Now that spring's returned, I like to get up early.
Reclusive living soothes the tattered soul.

Replace the stones of a caved-in wall,
thin trees for a view of the mountains.

On hands and knees, I clear a trail,
hidden, snaking up a hill—

then see my servant boy returning:
cold wine in a huge clay jar.

To a Guest

Spring waters run north and south from here,
but we have only the gulls for guests.

Now you've climbed our bramble path
and entered our rough wood gate.

This far from town, our cooking isn't fancy.
Stale rice wine is all a poor man has to offer.

Sit here. I'll fetch my ancient neighbor
to come and help us drink it.

Homestead

My homestead lies beside a clear stream,
its wicker gate on an unused road.

Deep grass hides it from the marketplace.
It's so secluded, I don't even have to dress.

Branch upon branch, the willows droop:
Tree after tree, the loquats still smell sweet.

Sunset reflects the fishing cormorants
drying their beautiful black wings.

In Seclusion

It is evening before I rise.
Out of work, I find the house is peaceful.

Bamboo surrounds the wilds
and the water reflects my cottage.

My sons are lazy boors,
my wife complains of constant poverty.

I'd like to be drunk a hundred years.
It's already been a month since I even combed my hair.

The Madman

My house lies west of Thousand Mile Bridge
near Hundred Flower Creek

where this old recluse delights:
each green bamboo in the wind

trembles like a girl, each red blossom
of the lotus adds perfume.

Old friends have joined the bourgeoisie
and no longer write me letters.

My children grow pale as ghosts
from the hunger. The Madman only laughs

before he drowns in the gutter—
growing older, I grow madder.

A Hundred Worries

Fourteen and still a boy,
I ran wild as a calf in spring.

When the pears were ripe in the autumn,
I climbed a thousand trees a day.

Now my fiftieth year approaches,
I grow sedentary and nap when I should walk.

Polite when I visit friends,
a hundred worries plague me.

At home, the rooms remain empty
and my wife understands my grief.

Our children won't bow to their father,
but weep for food in the barren kitchen.

Random Pleasures (V)

Grieved, I idle and doze
while spring sneaks up the river.

So why these numberless blossoms,
why do the orioles sound bitter?

Random Pleasures (VI)

The peach and plum I planted were my own.
Though low, my walls still mark my garden.

Spring winds still come to plunder:
at night they steal my blossoms.

Random Pleasures (VII)

River swallows know my shack is humble:
they come and go at random.

Mud nests in my scrolls, turds all over my lute,
they fly so close I can touch them!

Random Pleasures (VIII)

Unemployed and lazy, I hang around the village.
I leave my sons behind, beside the garden gate.

I take my rice to a mossy bed in the woods
to sleep out in the breeze that blows in from the lake.

Random Pleasures (IX)

West of my hut, I grow mulberry;
down by the river there is wheat.

How many times will I see spring turn into summer?
I cling to my honey-sweet rice wine.

Evening After Rain

The sudden wind brought rain this afternoon
to save my thirsty garden.

Now sunset steams the grass
and the river softly glistens.

Who'll organize my scattered books?
Tonight I'll fill and fill my glass.

I know they love to talk about me.
But no one faults me for my reclusive life.

Song for a Young General

Brocade threads and summer reeds
weave a tune of clouds and breezes.

How many times in one man's life
can he listen to Heaven's music?

After Solstice

After solstice, the sunlight slowly lengthens.
From Two-edged Sword Trail, my thoughts turn again to Lo-yang.

Neither robe of office nor big white horse mean a thing—
nor a valley of gold with bronze camels—so far from home.

Plum blossoms? I don't see a thing. Mountain cherry
                          and sweet bloom severed,
one aches, longing for the other like separated brothers.

Sorrows weigh me down when poems should touch the roots
                          of joy to rouse it,
but with each peom completed, chanting, the old, cold ache
                                    is started.

In Praise of Rain

We suffered drought, months without rain.
Then, this morning, clouds climbed from the river:

misty rain began to drizzle,
falling in every direction.

Birds returned to their nests,
forest flowers freshened all their colors.

Now, at dusk, the rains continue their song
and I want to hear it all night long.

Singing Girls (Written in Jest)

I.
The officials are quick to dismount,
welcomed by girls who greet the barges.
When these girls sing,
the river reflects their fans,
and when they dance,
their dresses touch the sand.
Their white sleeves luff in the wind,
wine jars bob in the waves.
How inviting as they compete with painted eyes,
rekindling youthful fires!

II.
Song and dance retired the blistering sun.
Now flute songs fill the sky.
Shining eyes dance a delicate chorus,
their headdresses sway in line.
Horses wait, rumps to the hills,
barges float a river of perfume.
Friend, your wife's at home alone:
stay away from wild ducks and drakes.

Clear After Rain

Long after rainfall, Sorceress Hills grow dark.
But now they brighten, stitched with gold and silver.

Green grass edges the darkening lake
and clouds stream red from the east.

All day long, the orioles call,
and cranes brush these tall white clouds.

Once dry, these wild flowers bend, and there
where the wind is sweeping, fall.

Poem for My Brother Returning to My Farm

Wandering has been my way,
and you alone stayed with me.

You knew the shortcuts by the streams,
the secret ways back home.

Count the ducks and geese at twilight
and latch the old wood gate.

When the bamboo grove is thin, plant more —
the season soon grows late.

Spring Homecoming

Through tall bamboo the mossy path
winds down to the easy river.

Flowers bloom beneath the eaves
of the ancient wide-thatched hall.

After months away,
I come back home in spring,

leaning on my cane
to look at flowers and stones,

packing my wine jar down
to walk and drink on the beach.

Gulls swim and dive in the distance,
swallows wrestle with the wind.

The world's ways are difficult, indeed,
but every life has its limits.

Sobering up, I drink again:
stoned, I finally feel at home.

Lone Wild Goose

Alone, the wild goose refuses food and drink,
his calls, searching for the flock.

Who feels compassion for that single shadow
vanishing in a thousand distant clouds?

You watch, even as it flies from sight,
its plaintive calls cutting through you.

The noisy crows ignore it:
the bickering, squabbling multitudes.

I Stand Alone

A falcon hovers at the edge of the sky.
Two gulls drift slowly up the river.

Vulnerable while they ride the wind,
they coast and glide with ease.

Dew is heavy on the grass below,
the spider's web is ready.

Heaven's ways include the affairs of man:
among a thousand sorrows, I stand alone.

The Thatched Hut

When Barbarians overran the city,
I abandoned my old thatched hut.

But now the city is peaceful once again,
and at last I can come back.

The rebellion broke in a flash—
planned to be ruthless and sudden.

With our general off to visit the Court,
his hirelings conspired,

they sacrificed a beautiful white stallion
and swore their oath in its blood.

Some rode west to conscript our army;
some closed the road to the north;

some, particularly vile,
even named themselves to office.

But when Barbarians challenged them for power,
these traitors were afraid.

In the west, the army mutinied,
rebel killing rebel—

who could have guessed their deaths
would come from their own cruel legions—

and all decent people grieved
at a world plunged into chaos.

Petty officials multiplied,
and thousands became their victims.

Their terrorist hirelings, indiscriminate,
murdered innocent and innocent alike,

amused themselves with torture
performed to chamber music,

and ordered death with a laugh.
The streets were sewers of blood.

You still can hear their cries
there where the axes fell.

The rebels plundered freely,
stealing horses, enslaving women,

and where was the Empire then?
We were afraid and broken-hearted.

I had no choice—I ran.
And longed three years for the coast.

Arrows filled the air above the Yangtze.
And I longed for the Five Lakes region.

A life away is not a life—
I return to attack my weeds.

Inside the gate, my four strong pines.
I stroll through my bamboo grove.

My old dog yips and leaps,
darting in and out of my robe.

My neighbors rush out to greet me
with bottles of sweet rice wine.

Even the governor sends greetings
by an official to assess my needs.

Our whole village celebrates,
my neighbors and my friends,

but there's still no peace in the world.
We honor more soldiers than poets.

Between the wind and the dust,
is there room for a poor man's life?

I live like a parasite—
happily, happy just to be alive.

If I've not earned my food and wine,
let all the worst be mine.

After the Harvest

The rice is cut and clouds glisten in the fields.
Facing Stone Gate, the river is low.

Winds shriek, ripping leaves from shrubs and trees.
At dawn, the pigs and chickens scatter.

Out of the distance, I hear the first sounds of battle.
The woodcutter's song is over. Soon he will leave the village.

Homeless and old, I long for a word from the homeland.
A wanderer, I place my trust in the world.

細草微風岸　危檣獨夜舟
星垂平野闊　月湧大江流
名豈文章著　官應老病休
飄飄何所似　天地一沙鷗

丙寅暮春錄杜甫旅夜書懷於懷玉堂　謝璞

Night Thoughts While Traveling

Thin grass bends on the breezy shore,
and the tall mast seems lonely in my boat.

Stars ride low across the wide plain,
and the moon is tossed by the Yangtze.

What is fame and literary status—
the old and infirm should leave office.

Adrift, drifting, what is left for a lone gull
adrift between earth and heaven.

Running from Trouble

Barely fifty, but already my face is old, my hair white.
I traveled this whole coast fleeing from The State.

Rough cloth saved my shivering bones
as I roamed the awful cold.

Thus began the years of my disease.
Everywhere, the people were mud and ashes.

Between heaven and earth,
there's nowhere a body is safe.

I see my wife and children follow.
We sigh for mutual sorrows.

My old home gone to weeds,
and all my neighbors scattered,

we may never find the road back home.
We weep our eyes dry in the river.

A Broken Boat

All my life, I've dreamed of lakes and rivers.
I've had that little boat for years.
I used to row in the creek every day
out beyond my brushwood gate.

But then I fled the rebellion
and longed for my hut in these hills.
My neighbors all have vanished,
and now the bamboo groves are tall.

With my boat a year in the water,
I don't dare tap on the bottom.
Other travelers go west on easy wings.
Even the river moves easily, flowing east.

I could repair my poor old boat,
or I could easily buy another.
Why have I always run from trouble?
Even in my cottage, there's no peace.

Facing the Snow

New ghosts weep over lost battles.
Alone and old, I recite a litany of woes.

Heavy clouds rumble into the sunset,
quick snow dancing in the winds.

Imperfect, the smith's new ladle lies discarded,
but his fire still throbs red.

No news. Are all the provinces still there?
I write out my sorrows in air.

Traveler's Pavilion

Sunrise brightens my autumn window.
Winds have once again stripped trees.

The morning sun slips between cold mountains,
and the river runs through last night's mist.

Our court makes use of everything it can,
but what's the use of a sick old man?

And what of my one life remains,
rising or falling on autumn winds.

On a Portrait of a Falcon

Wind and frost on ordinary silk,
and this wonderful gray falcon.

Body tensed, he eyes a rabbit,
watching his flanks as well.

On a ring the size of a finger,
he hangs, waiting for a call.

Oh, he will bring down the little birds
leaving feathers and blood on the plains.

Homage to the Painter General Ts'ao

As Lady Wei's star pupil, your calligraphy
was compared to General Wang's.

Impervious to old age, when you painted,
prosperity slipped past you like clouds.

Sleepless Nights

The bamboo cold creeps into my room.
Moonlight over the wilds floods the yard.

The dew grows heavy, dripping,
and only here and there some stars.

Fireflies shine their own lights, flying the dark.
Perched birds call out across the water.

The world's affairs are snarled in war.
I regret the night is wasted.

Night in a Room by the River

Evening rises toward the mountain trails
as I climb up to my high chamber.

Thin clouds lodge along the cliffs.
A lonely moon rocks slowly on the waves.

A line of cranes flaps silently over,
and, far off, a howling pack of wolves.

Sleepless, memories of war betray me:
I am powerless against the world.

Six Choruses

1.

The sun rises over eastern seas,
clouds rise over the muddy northlands.
Kingfishers sing from the tall bamboo.
Egrets dance on the sand.

2.

Mist drifts down as the flowers fall;
butterflies and bees all rise.
What should I do if someone comes
to visit in the shade where I roost?

3.

Dig a well and make a rope of hemp,
and bamboo pipes for drainage.
The boats are knotted at their mooring.
Crooked pathways bind the village.

4.

Rains falls at the river mouth,
low sun embraces the willows.
Dark birds meet near broken nests;
a white fish leaps from grass floating in the river.

5.

Bamboo overtakes this hut's poor walls
and cane blooms in the courtyard eaves.
The river takes the sun's soft strands
to weave with slender reeds.

6.

The moon floats across a river of sky,
but this river is illusion—a cloud of mist in flowers.
The silent roosting bird understands the Tao:
sails don't know where they go.

Moon, Rain, Riverbank

Rain roared through, now the autumn night is clear.
The water wears a patina of gold
and carries a bright jade star.
Heavenly River runs clear and pure,
as gently as before.

Sunset buries the mountains in shadow.
A mirror floats in the deep green void,
its light reflecting the cold, wet dusk,
dew glistening,
freezing on the flowers.

A Summit

Biting winds, dark clouds, monkeys howling in the trees.
Gulls circle slowly over sands.

Crumple of windblown fallen leaves.
The river laps at the shore.

Always, in autumn, away from home,
I endure this long, steep climb.

Sick and alone, failure turned my temples snowy.
I suffer and I grumble: giving up the wine.

To My Young Brother
(of whom I've learned nothing
in four years' time)

I've heard from strangers you may be living
in a Hangchou mountain temple.

The dusty winds of war prolong our separation,
and now I've spent another autumn beside the Yangtze and the Han.

My shadow passes under trees filled with screaming monkeys,
but my heart turns down toward the dragons at the river-mouth.

When spring waters rise, may they carry me down
to search for you in the East where the white clouds end.

By Yangtze and Han

Wandering beside rivers, I remember my home
between heaven and earth, an aging exiled scholar.

Only a smeared ghost of a cloud
and a pale moon in the long night sky.

The sun has set in my heart.
Autumn winds rise up around my sickbed.

Even the old horse has its stall in the barn
though he's too old for the road.

At the Thatched Hall of the Ts'ui Family

It is autumn at the grass hut on Jade Peak.
The air is cool and clear.

Temple bells and chimes echo from the canyons.
Fishermen and woodsmen wind over sunset trails.

We fill our plates with chestnuts gathered in the valley
and rice grown in the village.

For what, Wang Wei?
Bamboo and pine, silent, locked behind a gate.

春岸桃花水云帆枫树林偷生长避地适远更沾襟老病南征日君恩北望心百年歌自苦未见有知音

桂省南征 谢瑾书

Heading South

Spring returns to Peach Blossom River
and my sail is a cloud through maple forests.

Exiled, I lived for years in secret, moving on
farther from home with tear-stains on my sleeves.

Now old and sick, at last I'm headed south.
Remembering old friends, I look back north a final time.

A hundred years I sang my bitter song,
but not a soul remembers those old rhymes.

Facing the Snow (II)

Northern snows invade the city,
northern clouds have frozen all the homes.

Hard winds mix leaves with snow,
cold rains erase the flowers.

Once again, no money. I wonder
if I could get wine on credit.

But without a friend to share it,
I'll wait for sunset and the crows.